BANBURY TO BIRMINGHAM

Vic Mitchell and Keith Smith

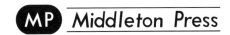

MP Middleton Press

Cover picture: Having climbed continuously for seven miles, class 9F 2-10-0 no. 92008 reaches a short downhill section as its southbound wagons rattle through Southam Road & Harbury on 19th April 1963. (P.J.Garland/R.S.Carpenter)

Published March 2004

ISBN 1 904474 27 6

© *Middleton Press, 2004*

Design   *David Pede*
Typesetting   *Barbara Mitchell*

Published by

       Middleton Press
       Easebourne Lane
       Midhurst, West Sussex
       GU29 9AZ

Tel: 01730 813169
Fax: 01730 812601
Email: info@middletonpress.co.uk
www.middletonpress.co.uk

Printed & bound by MPG Books Ltd, Bodmin, Cornwall

INDEX

ACKNOWLEDGEMENTS

We are grateful to many of those mentioned in the credits for their assistance and also to I.Baxter, A.E.Bennett, W.R.Burton, L.Crosier, G.Croughton, F.Hornby, J.B.Horne, M.A.N.Johnston, N.Langridge, D.T.Rowe, B.Lewis, Mr D. & Dr S.Salter, G.T.V.Stacey, R.E.Toop, P.Q.Treloar, R. Whateley, E.Wilmshurst, D.Wilson and finally our wives, Barbara Mitchell and Janet Smith.

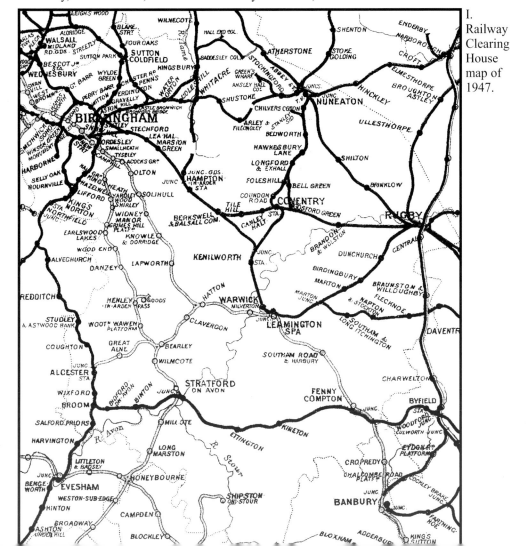

I. Railway Clearing House map of 1947.

GEOGRAPHICAL SETTING

The old established market town of Banbury is situated on the south flowing River Cherwell, close to which runs our route for its first five miles. The town is on the Lower Lias Limestone of the northern extension of the Cotswold Hills and the line was built on this outcrop for its southern 15 miles. There were deposits of ironstone of economic importance in this vicinity.

The route drops off these formations and traverses mainly Keuper Marl for the remainder of its length. It dips between Leamington Spa and Warwick to cross the only watercourse of note on its length, the south flowing River Avon. The geology gives rise to good arable and pasture land, but on the approach to Birmingham much of this has been used for housing. The density increases from Solihull northwards.

The journey north of Hatton is at 300-400ft above sea level, an altitude unfamiliar to most residents of Southeast England.

The maps are to the scale of 25ins to 1 mile with north at the top, unless otherwise indicated.

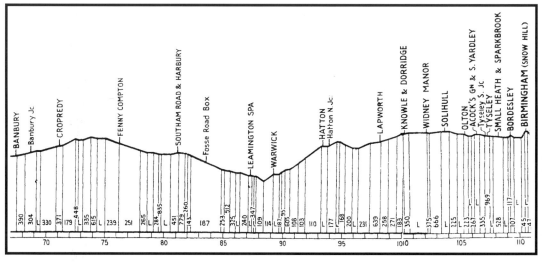

II. Gradient profile with mileage from London.

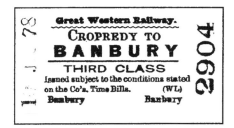

HISTORICAL BACKGROUND

The Great Western Railway's route was completed between London and Birmingham when the line north of Banbury came into use on 1st October 1852. It was laid to the broad gauge of 7ft 0¼ins, but standard gauge rails were added and used exclusively after 1st April 1869.

Branches opened westward to Stratford upon Avon in 1860 (from Hatton) and to Henley in Arden in 1894. The latter was closed to passengers in 1915 and to goods in 1917.

A more direct route between Stratford upon Avon and Birmingham was opened southwards from Tyseley in 1907, this reducing traffic on the main line north of Hatton. It was this that made the Henley in Arden branch redundant.

In anticipation of an increase in London expresses due to the shortening of the line south of Banbury in 1910, part of the route was quadrupled; Tyseley to Olton was completed on 27th January 1907, Olton to Lapworth followed on 28th May 1933.

The GWR became the Western Region of British Railways upon nationalisation on 1st January 1948. The route was transferred to the London Midland Region in September 1963. Consequent to privatisation in 1996, trains have been operated over the full length of the route by Chiltern Railways and Virgin Cross Country. Thames Trains worked Stratford upon Avon services south of Hatton, while Central Trains operated all local services north of Leamington Spa.

PASSENGER SERVICES

The initial service comprised six trains, weekdays only; down trains are considered in this section. By 1869, the figure was the same, but there were six more north of Leamington Spa and three through trains on Sundays.

The table gives the number of expresses calling at both ends of the route, plus principal intermediate stations in most cases. Stopping trains, mostly serving only the northern part of the route, are also listed.

	Express		Local	
	Weekdays	Sunday	Weekdays	Sundays
1880	1	0	18	8
1901	5	0	28	11
1920	7	2	32	9
1940	11	5	36	8

For much of the post war period, there were eight regular expresses, but this figure increased to 14 in 1960-66, during the period of the upgrading of the Euston-Birmingham line. The diesel Blue Pullman was a notable feature of the route in 1960-67.

Introduction of diesel local services in 1957 brought improved frequencies north of Leamington Spa, but a sparse service south thereof. The latter ceased at the end of 1964.

A good frequency has been maintained on the northern section subsequently, with even further increases in express numbers, notably from the South Coast and London Marylebone. The latter was hourly in 2003, when plans were being made to halve this interval.

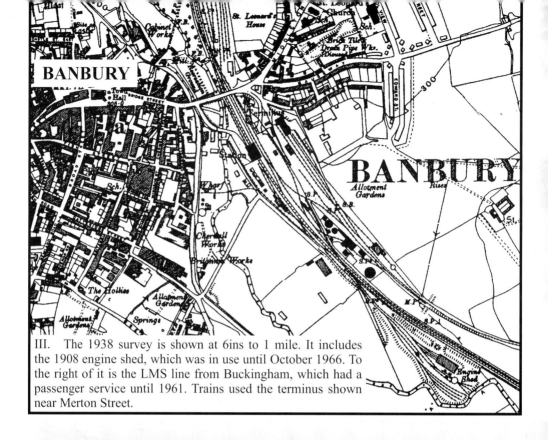

III.   The 1938 survey is shown at 6ins to 1 mile. It includes the 1908 engine shed, which was in use until October 1966. To the right of it is the LMS line from Buckingham, which had a passenger service until 1961. Trains used the terminus shown near Merton Street.

1.   This southward view features the overall roof which survived until 1952. There are also many of the original tall chimney pots, but they did not last to the end. The local train is waiting in one of the three bay platforms that were added in 1903. (Lens of Sutton coll.)

2.   Looking north from the up platform in 1950, we can see the poor state of the roof. Plans had been made in 1938 to reconstruct the entire station, but they were delayed by the advent of World War II. Note the short length of the down platform. (LGRP/NRM)

3.　The main entrance was (and is) on the down side and appears on the left of the previous picture. It is seen in 1953 in the company of an Austin 10. The busy station suffered the handicap of having only two through platforms. (C.B.Swallow/M.J.Stretton coll.)

4.　The long awaited rebuilding was well advanced when photographed in June 1957, concrete being the principal material used. The central heating chimney is in the background of this and the next picture. (G.Adams/M.J.Stretton coll.)

5.　The completed station is seen from the north as a Pressed Steel DMU draws out after arrival as the 4.18pm from Paddington on 6th August 1960. It will move to the platform behind no. 6931 *Aldborough Hall*, before returning to London. The bay to the left of the DMU was used by Eastern Region trains to Woodford Halse until 5th September 1966 and it lost its track in 1969. (M.Mensing/M.J.Stretton coll.)

Gt Western Ry	Gt.'Western Ry
BANBURY	BANBURY
TO	8.9
PADDINGTON	
ViaBicester&Beaconsfld	
THIRD CLASS	
8/5 **Fare** 8/5	
Issued subject to the conditions&regulations set out in theCompanys Time Tables Bills& Notices	
Paddington	Paddington

3943　3943

Gt Western Ry	Gt Western Ry
BANBURY	BANBURY
TO	S.23
LEAMINGTON SPA	
THIRD CLASS	
2/6 **Fare** 2/6	
Issued subject to the conditions&regulations set out in the Company'sTime Tables Bills&Notices	
Leamington Spa	Leamington Spa

7849　7849

6. One of the Blue Pullmans was recorded after arrival from London at platform 3 on 30th August 1962. These diesel units were in use on the route from 1960 to 1967. No. 6929 *Whorlton Hall* was station pilot that day and is at platform 2. Refreshment facilities were provided on the footbridge and also in the lofty entrance hall. (B.S.Jennings)

7. No. 165206 arrives at platform 3 at 12.43 on 11th June 2002, while running from Birmingham Snow Hill to Marylebone. The bay was no longer numbered and accommodated no. 47726 on standby duties. The station was still in as-built condition and the up goods line passed to the east of it. (V.Mitchell)

8. No. 5001 *Llandovery Castle* waits to depart north with the 1.10pm Paddington to Wolverhampton on 9th September 1962. The lineside clocks were an unusual feature of the rebuilding of the station. All expresses were diesel hauled after that day. The station had the suffix "General" from 1938 to 1961. (B.S.Jennings)

NORTH OF BANBURY

9.   The following views are from the bridge seen in pictures 7 and 8. They include Banbury North box which was fitted with a 95-lever frame and was still in use a century after the station was first rebuilt in 1903. Five dead-end sidings were laid on the right in 1884, but they became part of a hump marshalling yard in 1931. The photo is from May 1933. (Brunel University/Mowat coll.)

10.   The yard could accommodate 2000 wagons, but it ceased to be used for its intended purpose on 4th May 1970. It is seen on 1st October 1975 as no. 47351 runs south with oil tanks. The site of the brake van siding (centre) is covered with grass and by 1994, housing was spreading across the site. The yard was used for exchange of traffic between the Eastern and Western Regions. (T.Heavyside)

11.   The small shunt signal is off to allow a DMU to pass behind the signal box before reversing to the station to form the 15.51 to Marylebone on 11th May 1986. The Oxford Canal is on the left. (S.P.Derek)

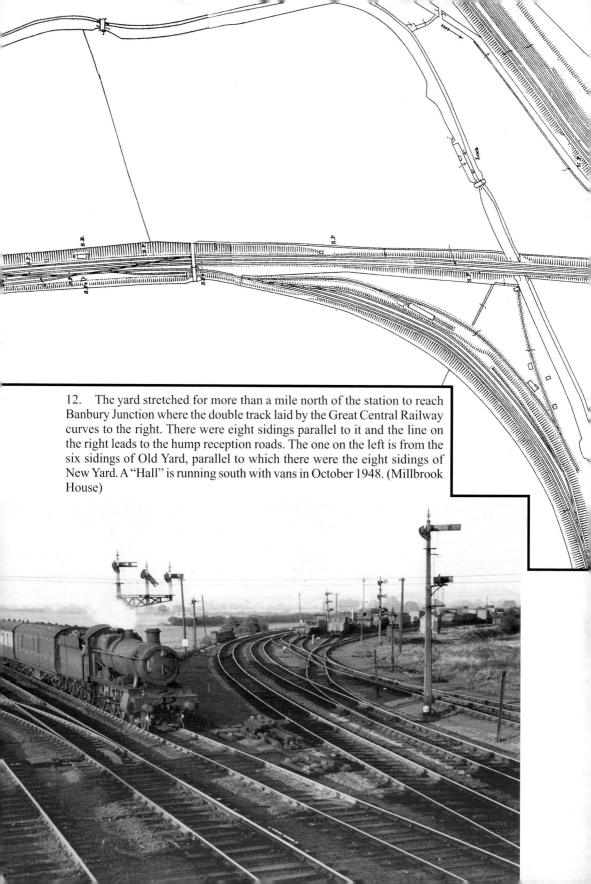

12.   The yard stretched for more than a mile north of the station to reach Banbury Junction where the double track laid by the Great Central Railway curves to the right. There were eight sidings parallel to it and the line on the right leads to the hump reception roads. The one on the left is from the six sidings of Old Yard, parallel to which there were the eight sidings of New Yard. A "Hall" is running south with vans in October 1948. (Millbrook House)

IV.   Our route is from right to left on this 1922 map which is at 15ins to 1 mile; the GCR branches east at the top. Curving west on the left page is the Oxfordshire Ironstone Company's line. On the right page is the 98-lever Banbury Junction box, which functioned until 24th April 1980. On the left is Banbury Ironstone Branch box, which had 49 levers and was in use from 8th February 1920 until 13th April 1969.

13.   Chiltern Railways "Clubman" no. 168001 runs from Birmingham to London on 19th May 2000 and passes the site of the hump yard (foreground). Derbyshire stone is being unloaded at Redland's stone terminal. There are goods loops each side of the running lines. (M.Turvey)

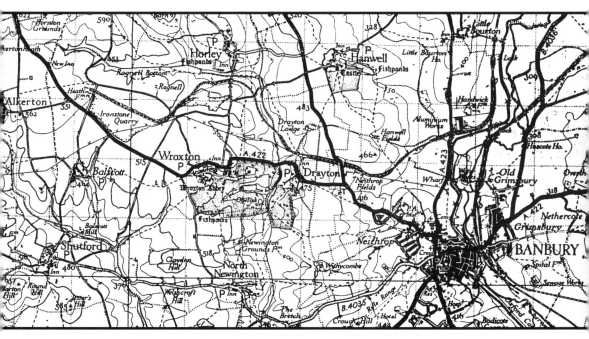

V.   The 1917 company was owned jointly by three of the biggest iron and steel producers in Britain and 2m tons of ore were often dug here annually. The five route miles are shown across this 1ins to 1 mile map of 1945. The LNER line is on the right.

14.   The system opened in 1919 and the main line was gradually doubled. The engine shed headquarters and workshops at Wroxton were photographed on 15th September 1956, along with examples of the fleet of 0-4-0STs and 0-6-0STs, the latter being used on the longer journeys. There was another engine shed at Pinhill Farm and there were two signal boxes at level crossings. (H.Davies)

15. A closer view of the signal box shows that it bears the loco crew roster. There were about 20 steam locomotives in the fleet, the last being purchased in 1958. Seen here is *Barabel*, a 1953 Hudswell Clarke 0-4-0ST. (H.Davies)

16. Assorted hopper wagons were waiting to be loaded at Wroxton on 17th May 1958. The steam locomotives were replaced by new Sentinel diesels in 1964, but the entire system was closed on 30th September 1967. On the left is 1941 Peckett *Allan* and nearby is 1952 Hunslet *Alex*. (B.Roberts/A.Neale coll.)

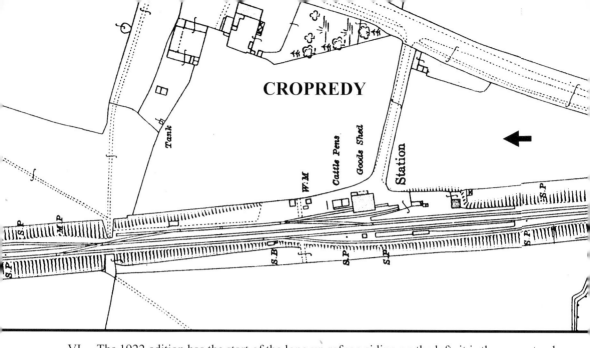

CROPREDY

VI. The 1922 edition has the start of the long up refuge siding on the left; it is the upper track. The lower one on the right is the down goods loop.

17. This view north features the large goods shed, traffic here justifying the employment of ten men throughout the 1930s. The photograph is from May 1933, but no traces remain today. (Brunel University/Clinker coll.)

18. This southward panorama is from 1952, at which time there were down departures at 1.58pm on Saturdays and 4.52pm Mondays to Saturdays. The up trains were at 10.28am and 3.6pm, both on weekdays only. (LGRP/NRM)

19.   On the right is the down goods loop, which began at Banbury and was in use to this point from 1915 until 13th April 1969, when this 19-lever signal box closed. It was photographed just prior to closure, along with the contrasting signal posts. The next box north was at Claydon Crossing; it had 21 levers and was open from 1901 to 1980. (Lens of Sutton coll.)

20.   Wagons stand on the 1898 up refuge siding as Sulzer diesel electric no. D5197 roars north on 27th September 1965. The signal box is barely visible in the distance. The station lost its passenger service on 17th September 1956 and goods traffic ended on 4th May 1964. (M.Mensing/M.J.Stretton coll.)

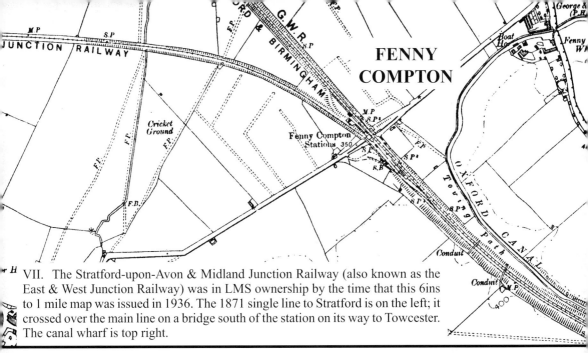

FENNY COMPTON

VII. The Stratford-upon-Avon & Midland Junction Railway (also known as the East & West Junction Railway) was in LMS ownership by the time that this 6ins to 1 mile map was issued in 1936. The 1871 single line to Stratford is on the left; it crossed over the main line on a bridge south of the station on its way to Towcester. The canal wharf is top right.

21.   No. 3835 *County of Devon* is running south with a fish train and is passing the down platform. This had been built in 1902; the original one had been further south, opposite the up one. There were 9 or 10 men here between the wars and the LMS station master was in charge of both stations from 1929. (LGRP/NRM)

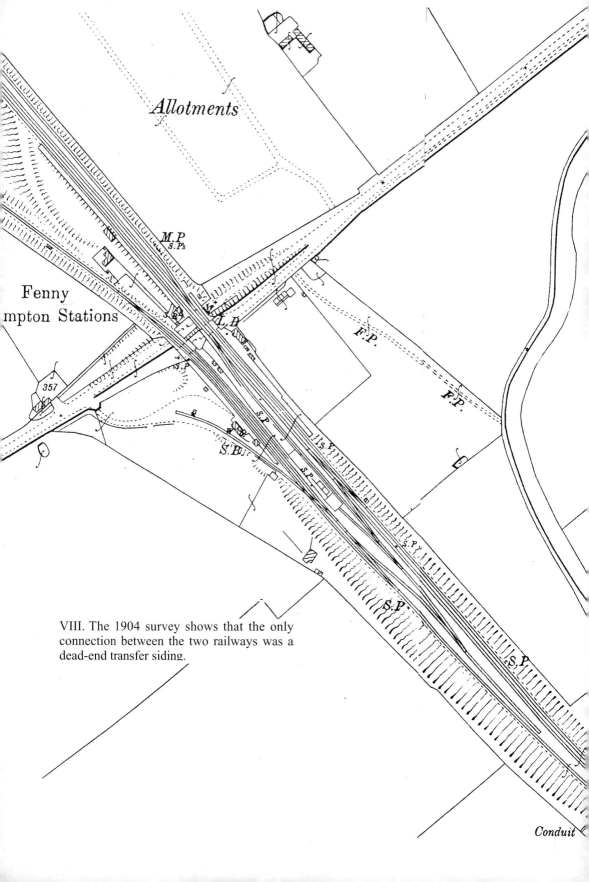

Allotments

M.P
S.Ps

Fenny
mpton Stations

L.B

357

F.P.

F.P.

S.B.

VIII. The 1904 survey shows that the only
connection between the two railways was a
dead-end transfer siding.

S.P.

Conduit

22.   Running north on 15th March 1952 is no. 4987 *Brockley Hall*. It is on the bridge over the lane. There was restricted headroom and so a parallel level crossing was provided for tall vehicles. The span on the left carried a footway, which led to a crossing to the down platform. There was also access from the road via steps. (H.C.Casserley)

23.   No. 5317 is near the up platform on the same day. The first down platform had been in the foreground and was moved to make way for lengthening the siding which served the cattle dock. The road ran to the goods shed; this yard closed in April 1958. The signal box was in use from June 1931 until 7th March 1960. It contained an LMS frame of 20 levers and a GWR one of 29 levers. (H.C.Casserley)

24. Passenger service ceased on the east-west route on 7th April 1952, but the associated sidings were in use until 4th May 1964. The former westbound platform is on the left. The other one had been removed in 1960 to make space for an additional track and a direct connection to the main line for iron traffic from the west. The signal box was also completed in 1960. The station on the main line closed to passengers on 2nd November 1964. (Lens of Sutton coll.)

25. We now have two photographs from 14th August 2003 and this shows that the 1960 signal box was still controlling mechanical equipment. The then new Virgin Voyagers passed very few semaphore signals. No. 220022 is forming the 12.56 Manchester Piccadilly to Reading. (M.J.Stretton)

26.   A northward panorama from the box has the main lines on the right. Those on the left converge
in the distance and continue four miles to Kineton to serve a massive military depot. Trains out of
traffic are often stored within its secure perimeter. There is an up loop (right), beyond which had
been Knighcote Box, which had four levers and was in use from 1900 to 1953. The branch diverges
from the down loop and has three tracks (left), running as far as the curve. (M.J.Stretton)

Fenny Compton	1903	1913	1923	1933
Passenger tickets issued	14959	14948	13608	5100
Season tickets issued	*	*	54	44
Parcels forwarded	10226	9510	7269	2181
General goods forwarded (tons)	1065	888	389	25
Coal and coke received (tons)	4	-	99	35
Other minerals received (tons)	460	474	330	49
General goods received (tons)	461	1077	555	423
Trucks of livestock handled	514	560	318	120
(* not available.)				

NORTH OF FENNY COMPTON

27.   About three miles from Fenny Compton was Greaves Siding box (28 levers. 1918-83). The cement works sidings had been on the west side of the line since 1878, although initially used for lime. From 1907, a down goods loop ran from there to the bridge seen in picture 28. A picture from September 1950 shows APCM Blue Circle's 1919 Peckett *Whitby* in use. Cement manufacture ceased about 20 years later, but the site was retained for distribution and a Fowler diesel was used for this traffic. (K.J.Cooper/A.Neale coll.)

IX.   A 3ft gauge system was used in the quarry and steam haulage was employed until two large 2-4-0 diesels were purchased from Fowlers in 1938.

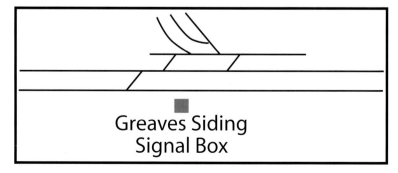

Greaves Siding
Signal Box

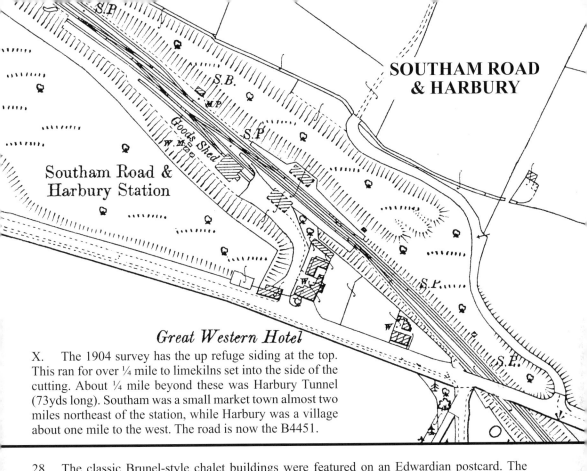

SOUTHAM ROAD & HARBURY

Southam Road &
Harbury Station

Great Western Hotel

X. The 1904 survey has the up refuge siding at the top. This ran for over ¼ mile to limekilns set into the side of the cutting. About ¼ mile beyond these was Harbury Tunnel (73yds long). Southam was a small market town almost two miles northeast of the station, while Harbury was a village about one mile to the west. The road is now the B4451.

28. The classic Brunel-style chalet buildings were featured on an Edwardian postcard. The number of employees in 1913 was 13; the figure rose to 18 in 1931. Two miles north of the station there were up and down goods loops at Fosse Road, from 1950 to 1976. (Lens of Sutton)

29.   Public goods traffic ceased on 11th November 1963, but over a million tons were recorded in some four year periods between the wars. A "Hall" 4-6-0 speeds south with an express in about 1955. The 33-lever box closed on 2nd April 1967. (J.H.Moss/R.S.Carpenter)

Gt Western Ry   Gt Western Ry
PRIVILEGE TICKET
Fenny Compton   Fenny Compton
TO
LEAMINGTON SPA
THIRD CLASS
5½d C Fare 5½d C
Leamington Spa.   Leamington Spa.
FOR CONDITIONS SEE BACK   W.D

397   397

2nd · SINGLE   SINGLE · 2nd
Southam Road & Harbury to
Southam Rd. & H.   Southam Rd. & H.
Leamington Spa G. Leamington Spa G.
LEAMINGTON SPA GENERAL
(W)   1/4 Fare 1/4   (W)
For conditions see Over For conditions see over

8494   8494

30. Passenger traffic ceased on 2nd November 1964, about ten years after this photograph was taken. It includes part of the up refuge siding and a notable taper on the signal post. The footbridge was added in about 1921. Another photograph appears on the cover of this volume. (P.J.Garland/R.S.Carpenter)

31. No. D1051 *Western Ambassador* is at the head of a Paddington to Wolverhampton express on 19th April 1963. Down trains called here at that time at 8.43am Mondays to Saturdays and at 2.58pm on Saturdays. The corresponding up trains were at 6.6pm and 2.14pm. The down goods loop is on the right; exit from this was controlled by a ground frame from 1967 to 1969. (P.J.Garland/R.S.Carpenter)

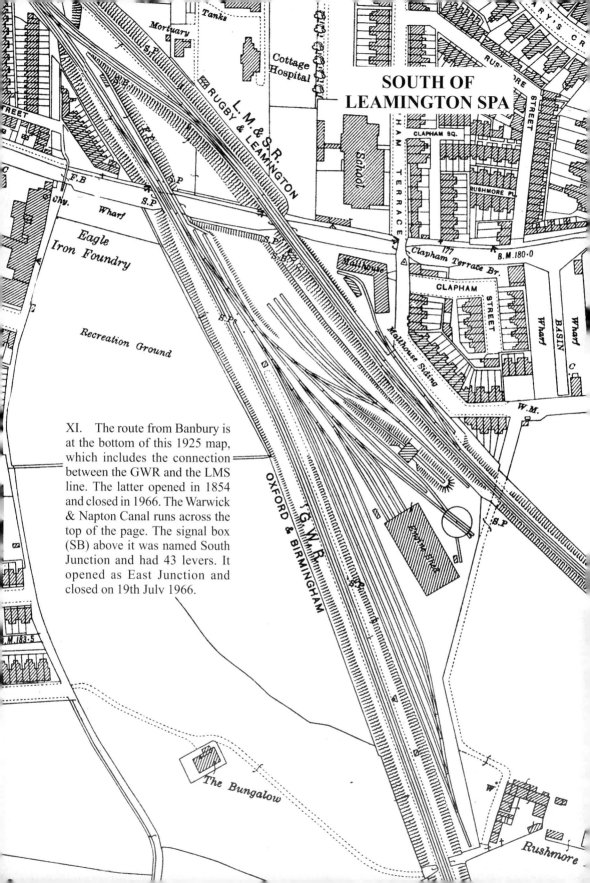

Mortuary

Tanks

Cottage Hospital

SOUTH OF LEAMINGTON SPA

L. M. & S.R.

RUGBY & LEAMINGTON

School

CLAPHAM SQ.

RUSHMORE STREET

RUSHMORE PL.

CLAPHAM TERRACE

177

B.M. 180·0

Clapham Terrace Br.

CLAPHAM

F.B

S.P.

Sdg.

Wharf

S.P.

Eagle Iron Foundry

S.P.

S.B.

Malthouse

CLAPHAM STREET

Wharf

WHARF BASIN

C.

Recreation Ground

B.P.

Malthouse Siding

W.M.

XI.   The route from Banbury is at the bottom of this 1925 map, which includes the connection between the GWR and the LMS line. The latter opened in 1854 and closed in 1966. The Warwick & Napton Canal runs across the top of the page. The signal box (SB) above it was named South Junction and had 43 levers. It opened as East Junction and closed on 19th July 1966.

OXFORD & BIRMINGHAM

G.W.R.

Engine Shed

S.P.

B.M. 183·5

The Bungalow

Rushmore

32. The original engine shed was north of the station; this more spacious depot was opened in September 1906 and was photographed on 27th April 1961. By that time its large allocation of 2-6-2Ts had diminished, owing to the advent of DMUs for the Birmingham services. Nos 8100 and 4118 are nearest. (P.J.Kelley)

33. A panorama from September 1963 includes the coal stage (left) and the carriage sidings. The shed housed only 17 locos by October 1959, this figure dropping to three prior to closure on 13th June 1965. The shed code was 84D until changed by the LMR to 2L in September 1963. The site is now occupied by an industrial estate. (R.S.Carpenter)

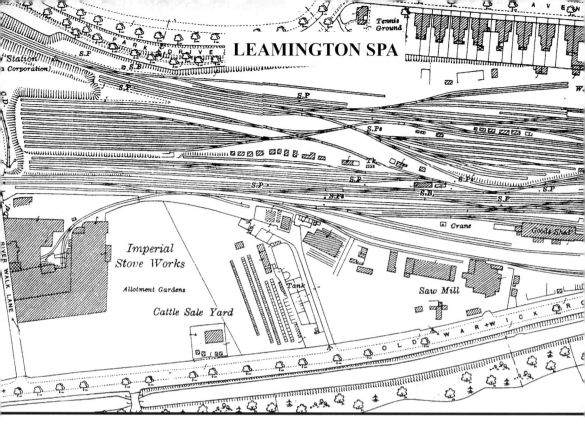

XII. The LMS route and its Avenue Station are above the GWR on this 1925 map, which is at 20ins to 1 mile. South Box is on the right page, near Lower Avenue, while North Box is on the left one, above the Saw Mill. Two cranes are shown; six tons could be lifted. Grabs were fitted for unloading vast quantities of coal for the gasworks, which was built near the canal (lower right) prior to the arrival of the GWR. The annual tonnage had exceeded 40,000 by 1940 and it increased further, but the works closed in 1964.

34.   The bridge over the High Street is in the background as a 3221 class 2-4-0 passes South Box with a down local train. The two lines on the left are goods loops. This and the next two pictures are from about 1910. (R.S.Carpenter coll.)

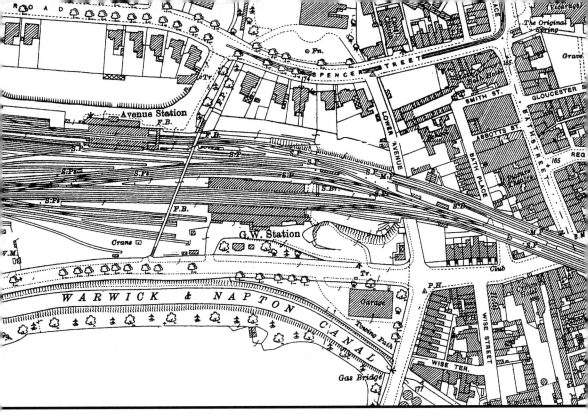

35.   A 151 "Chancellor" class 2-4-0 waits on the up goods loop having just used the single line connection between it and the London & North Western Railway. The LNWR horse box has a fodder compartment, as well as one for the groom, unlike the GWR model seen in the previous photo. (R.S.Carpenter coll.)

36.   The photographer is standing near the water column, seen in the last view, to record 2-4-2T no. 3609 with an up local train, probably from Birmingham. The staff level rose from 104 in 1913 to 160 in 1938. (R.S.Carpenter coll.)

Gt. Western Ry.   Gt. Western Ry.
WARWICK   WARWICK
TO
LEAMINGTON
4d. FIRST CLASS 4d.
Issued subject to the conditions and
regulations set out in the Company's
Time Tables, Bills and Notices.   F.N.
Leamington   Leamington

1454

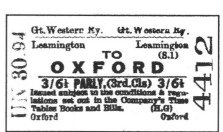

Gt. Western Ry.   Gt. Western Ry.
Leamington   Leamington
(8.1)
TO
OXFORD
3/6¼ PARLY.(3rd.Cls) 3/6¼
Issued subject to the conditions & regu-
lations set out in the Company's Time
Tables Books and Bills.   (H.G)
Oxford   Oxford

4412

37.   Both platforms had this unusual style of canopy, which was photographed in 1936, prior to the next major rebuilding; this is the up side. There seem to have been four tracks from at least 1880. (LGRP/NRM)

38.   The new exterior was recorded in 1947; the suffix "General" was in use from 1950 to 1968, "Spa" having been added in 1913. Queen Victoria granted the use of the prefix "Royal" in 1838, but it was not used by the railways. (A.W.V.Mace/Milepost 92½)

39.   The number 49447 was recorded by a group of observers as it took the down through line in about 1953. Such ex-LMS 0-8-0s were a common sight in the ensuing decade. Avenue Station closed to passengers on 18th January 1965. (A.W.V.Mace/Milepost 92½)

40.   A rare move was photographed on 3rd November 1962; a football special from Bournemouth to Coventry ran over the connection between the former rival systems. The roof of South Box is visible. It was closed on 19th July 1966. (S.C.Nash)

41. HSTs worked expresses between the North and South and also to Stratford upon Avon for many years. The "Wessex Scot" ran between Bournemouth and Edinburgh; the up and down services were recorded simultaneously on 15th May 1997. A new prototype panel box using solid state interlocking came into use near the junction on 8th August 1985. (M.J.Stretton)

42. The former LNWR route to Coventry curves left in the foreground. These connections came into use in May 1966 and all except the four lower sidings on the left of map XII were removed, along with all but three of those on the right of that page, north of North Box. These were retained for coal. Note that two bays were still in use when this photo was taken in June 2002. (V.Mitchell)

EAST OF WARWICK

43.   About one mile from both Leamington and Warwick, the line passes under three bridges, the centre one of which is an aqueduct carrying the Grand Union Canal. The signal is Leamington's up distant. (R.S.Carpenter coll.)

XIII. This 1925 extract is at 15ins to 1 mile and includes the sidings that were in use for the power station from 1920 to 1960, a canal aqueduct over the River Avon, the tramway depot and Warwick Avon Bridge box, which had a 22-lever frame and functioned from 30th September 1920 to 16th October 1966. Much of the area is now occupied by an electrical sub-station.

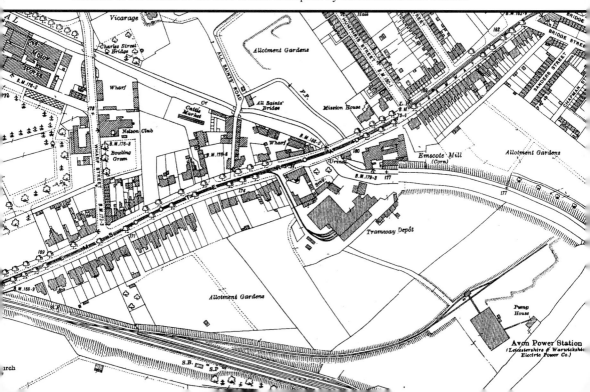

WARWICK

44.   No. 6363 is one of the 4300 class 2-6-0s and is seen with a down freight in the early 1950s.
The signal box had a 52-lever frame, which was worked from 1909 until 1969. The siding on the
right was often the refuge for banking engines waiting to help freight trains up the bank to Hatton.
(R.S.Carpenter coll.)

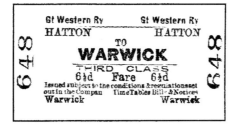

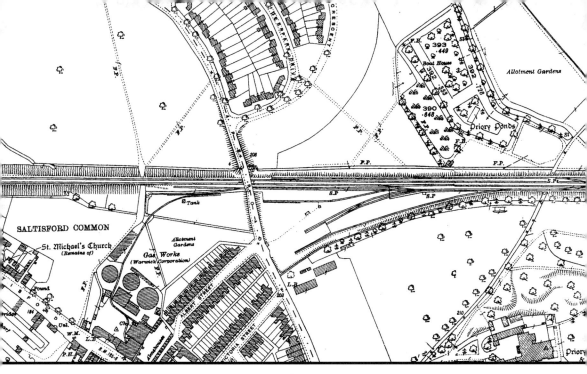

XIV. The 1925 map at 15ins to 1 mile has the station and original goods yard on the right page and the 1892 Cape Yard and gasworks sidings on the left. The second yard began life to serve a Royal Agricultural Society's show with two sidings. Four more were added later to those shown. The gasworks had a siding from about 1890; coal consumption increased from 5750 tons in1900 to 14,250 in 1947. Production ceased in about 1952. Both goods yards had a six-ton crane by 1938. Cape Yard was named after the locality and it closed on 11th November 1963, the main yard lasting until 31st January 1969.

45.   A westward view in 1963 includes the up refuge siding, which was a loop from 1944 to 1967. The bay was not for passenger use. There was a staff of about 30 for most of the 1930s. Warwick North box was about one mile distant and in use from 1942 to 1961. Its 25 levers controlled access to the sidings of a Government store on the up side. (P.J.Garland/R.S.Carpenter)

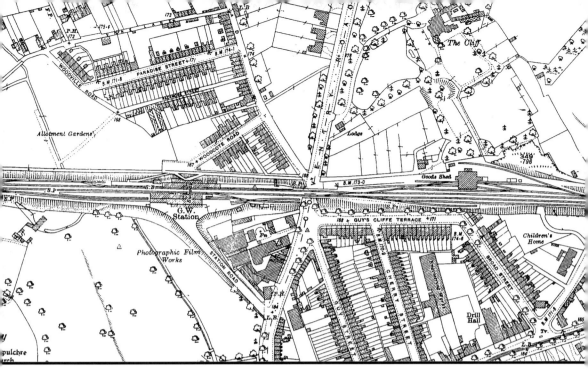

46. The down side building had a staffed ticket office when photographed in June 2002, but there was little weather protection for passengers, mere customers by that time. There was a crossover behind the camera, but it was little used. (V.Mitchell)

WARWICK PARKWAY

47. The new station was opened on 25th October 2001 by Chiltern Railways, but protection from the effects of skies of this type was of low priority. The down platform is on the right in this view from nine months after the opening. (V.Mitchell)

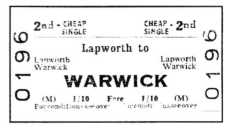

48.   Provision was made for the parking of 350 cars and the proximity of the A46(T) and the M40 facilitated access. Thankfully lifts were provided to the platforms. There was regular bus interchange and a staffed ticket office. (M.Turvey)

49.   Central Trains no. 150019 passes through, working a Leamington Spa to Kidderminster service on 22nd June 2003. There were hourly trains between Marylebone and Birmingham Snow Hill calling here. There had been a down loop and a 17-lever box at Budbrook, one mile to the west, until 1969. (M.Turvey)

HATTON

Hatton North Junction

OXFOR

G.W.R.
HATTON CURVE

Hatton Branch
Junction

R. AVON BRANCH

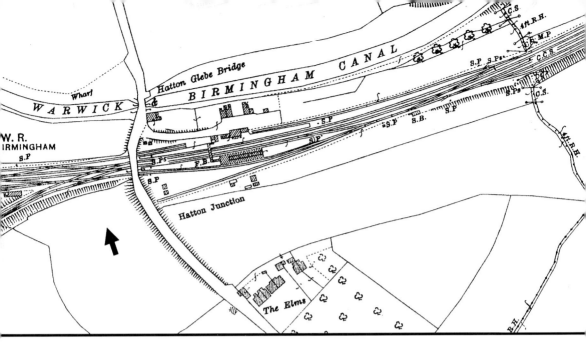

XV. The 1925 survey at 20ins to 1 mile has our route from right to left and the Stratford upon Avon line at the bottom. The canal is now known as the Grand Union. The Hatton Curve (left) came into use on 1st July 1897. There are four signal boxes shown: South, Middle, North and West. The first two lasted until 1936, when a new South Box was built on the down platform. Hatton or North Curve was singled in1968 and has subsequently had only a nominal service.

50.   The station became a junction on 9th October 1860 when the branch to Stratford upon Avon opened. This was built by an independent company, but operated by the GWR. This animated scene includes a Stratford train on the right and a horse box on the left. It is probably from the Edwardian era, when there was usually a staff of 17. (Stephenson Locomotive Society)

51. One of the second batch of GWR railcars is leaving the loop line towing a composite coach and is probably working a Stratford-Leamington Spa local service. (G.Adams/M.J.Stretton coll.)

52. A westward panorama from 1950 includes the earliest building, near the old coach body. This was used as a cycle shed. The branch became a through route to Worcester when the two temini in Stratford were linked on 24th July 1861, but such traffic ceased in 1966. There was a turntable on the left until 1913. (LGRP/NRM)

53. Two photographs from 13th September 1956 show the junction arrangements comprehensively. No.73025 was one of the BR class 5 4-6-0s introduced in 1951. (R.M.Casserley)

54. Middle Box had been near the pole on the left. Extra work for signalmen was generated by the many banking engines. The platform staff sometimes had to cope with around 200 fishermen returning from the canal at dusk on a Sunday. (R.M.Casserley)

55. The 84-lever South Box served until 1st September 1969, when the other two boxes also closed. Goods traffic was limited to one siding each side of the platforms, plus the dock in the foreground. Service ceased on 11th November 1963. The lighting was by petrol air gas, prior to electricity being introduced in 1949. The gas was produced in the shed on the left and the tall device helped to generate the pressure. Adjacent to the station were stores of the Royal Engineers. (Lens of Sutton)

56. Through trains to Worcester ceased on 3rd January 1966 and all the buildings were demolished not long afterwards. No. 47436 roars through with a train for Birmingham on 15th May 1976. A new ticket office is evident, but that did not last long. (T.Heavyside)

57. A photograph from 2002 reveals the arrangement that was introduced in 1968. Through trains from Paddington to Stratford upon Avon were increased from two to six in 1996 and all called here. There were two down sidings still in place beyond the platforms. (V.Mitchell)

LAPWORTH

XVI. The station opened in 1854 and was known as Kingswood until 1st May 1902. The goods yard together with up and down refuge sidings were added in 1888 and bay platforms were provided in 1894 for the Henley in Arden branch service. All these features are shown on this 1914 survey. The signal box marked S.B. was in use from 1894 to 1932. A pair of relief lines was laid from a crossover north of the station to Olton, and brought into use on 28th May 1933. Many new bridges had to be built on this eight-mile section.

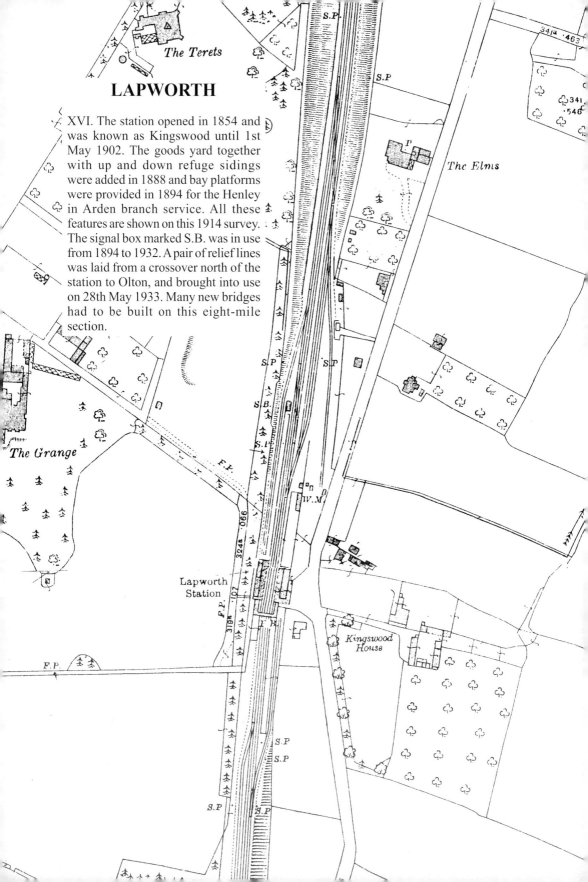

The Terets

The Elms

The Grange

Lapworth
Station

Kingswood
House

S.B.

W.M.

58. To the left of the up starting signal is one for Henley trains starting from the bay, which they did from 1894 to 1915. The service is referred to on the running-in board. The junction was almost two miles distant at Rowington, where there was a 25-lever signal box until October 1957. There were also water troughs in its vicinity. There were 10 or 11 men employed here in the 1920s. (Lens of Sutton coll.)

59. An autotrain arrives at the up platform and in the background is the goods yard. The final signal box, which saw service from June 1932 to September 1969, had a massive 78-lever frame. The train is probably bound for Henley in Arden. (Lens of Sutton coll.)

60.   No. 7247 is heading an up freight, which has just crossed from the relief to the main line on 5th October 1957. It is seen from the north end of the up platform with the connection to the goods yard on the right. The yard closed on 11th November 1963. (G.Adams/M.J.Stretton coll.)

────────►

61.   These tracks form a southward extension of the relief lines, but the one on which no. 5198 is standing ended at buffers behind the camera. Thus the platform acted as a bay for teminating trains from the north. There was an engine release crossover to the down main line to which the track on the left was also connected. These lines, plus the relief lines to Olton, were all abandoned in 1968. (J.W.T.House/C.L.Caddy)

────────►

62.   No. 153354 was recorded working the 16.10 Dorridge to Leamington Spa on 22nd April 1994. Regional Railways Central provided one service here in most hours at that time, but the trains usually started at Birmingham Snow Hill. (M.J.Stretton)

DORRIDGE

63. This northward postcard view was produced before the quadrupling in 1933. There were 15 to 16 men employed here between the wars. The roundhead windows were lost during the rebuilding. (Lens of Sutton coll.)

64. A northward panorama from 1952 from the up main platform confirms the concern that railway managers of the 1930s had for the comfort of their passengers. The 74-lever signal box was to the left of the camera until closure on 1st September 1969. (LGRP/NRM)

XVII. The 1925 survey shows four tracks at the top, but they converged to two after about ¼ mile. Of the four at the bottom, two converged and one was a siding. The station opened with the line as "Knowle". The suffix "& Dorridge" was added in 1897, but it reverted to just "Knowle" in 1968. It became plain "Dorridge" on 6th June 1974.

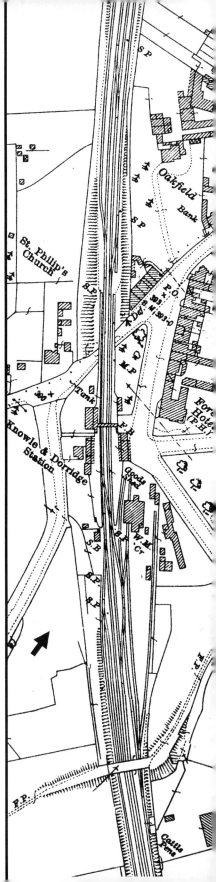

65.   No. 4170 was photographed in 1957 with a down local train on the relief line. This platform was taken out of use in 1968, but the adjacent one was retained, mainly for terminating trains. There were three carriage sidings south of the station until lifted in 1968. (J.W.T.House/C.L.Caddy)

66.   Two carriage sidings were formed from the redundant relief lines south of the platforms and this DMU has emerged from one of them to start its all-stations trip to Birmingham Moor Street on 15th May 1976. Some LMR officials may have delighted in reducing their former rival's route - even the roofing was removed here. (T.Heavyside)

67.   Chiltern Railways no. 165034 stands on the loop on 22nd June 2003 and was reported as working an all-stations service to Birmingham Snow Hill. Note that some weather protection had been provided again. (M.Turvey)

68.   When photographed in November 2003, the building was in good condition, inside and out. The photo was taken from the site of the goods yard, which had closed on 7th September 1964. MAT Transport used the carriage sidings for car loading for a period. (V.Mitchell)

NORTH OF DORRIDGE

XVIII. Up and down loops were brought into use in 1901 and an additional goods yard followed. The diagram shows the arrangement in 1937. There was a private siding near the word DOWN from 1943 to 1964 to serve a Ministry of Food cold store. After freight traffic ceased, the main sidings were retained for loading motor-vehicles. At the west end of the complex was Bentley Heath signal box which had a 49-lever frame in use from 1932 to 1969. The box was retained to control the level crossing, which was fitted with lifting barriers in 1973. "Crossing" was added to its name.

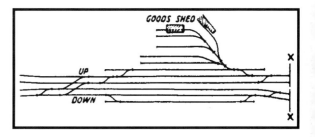

WIDNEY MANOR

69. The station opened on 1st July 1899 in rural surroundings and, as the maps show, residential development ensued. There were usually four men employed here for the first forty years. No. 5192 is southbound in 1957. (J.W.T.House/C.L.Caddy)

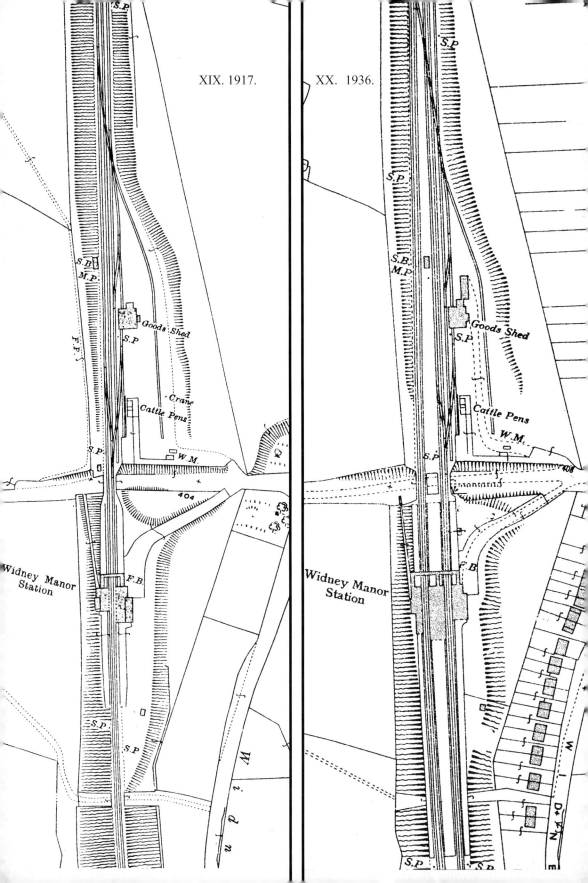

XIX. 1917.

XX. 1936.

S.P

S.P

S.P

S.B.
M.P.

S.B.
M.P.

Goods Shed

Goods Shed

S.P

S.P

Crane

Cattle Pens

Cattle Pens

W.M.

S.P

S.P

W.M.

404

Widney Manor
Station

404

Widney Manor
Station

F.B.

F.B.

S.P

S.P

M
i
p
u
n

S.P

S.P

S.P

70.   A panorama from the footbridge includes the cattle pens and rolling stock in the up refuge siding. This 1957 photo features 2-6-2T no. 5156; the leading two coaches are on the road bridge. Goods traffic ceased on 6th May 1963. (J.W.T.House/C.L.Caddy)

71.   Standard building plans were employed here, but no trace of the structures remains. In the distance is the signal box, which had 44 levers and closed on 1st September 1969. (Lens of Sutton coll.)

SOLIHULL

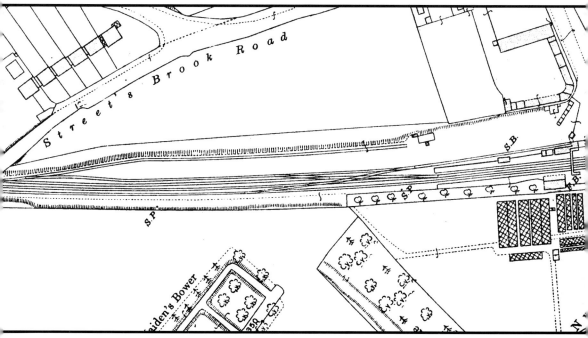

XXI. The 1917 edition includes long refuge sidings each side of the station. This layout dated from 1890. Prior to that time, the only sidings were the short ones, near the goods shed.

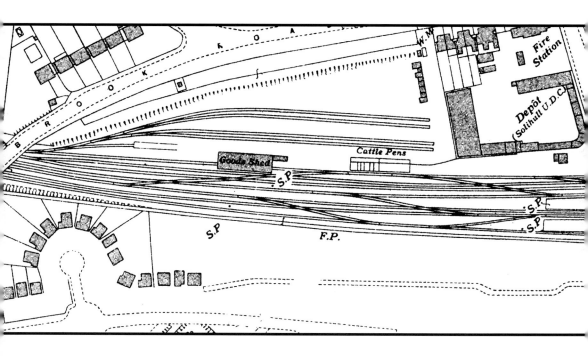

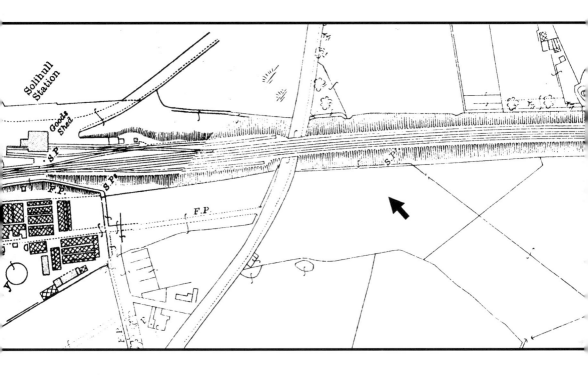

XXII.   The 1936 survey reveals that glasshouses were giving way to residential housing west of the line. The goods shed had been moved and the station had been totally rearranged.

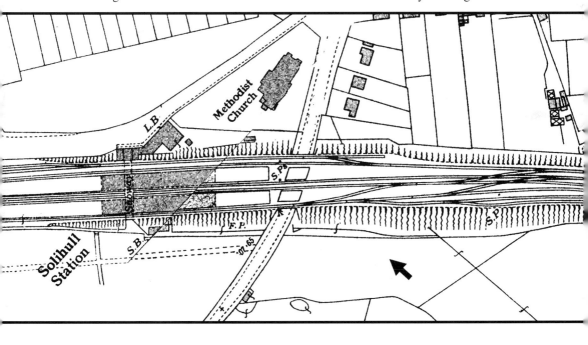

72. The chalet-style buildings favoured by Brunel stood until the 1933 quadrupling, when the footbridge was replaced by a long subway. There was a staff of 18 in that year. (Lens of Sutton)

73. No. 5950 *Wardley Hall* speeds north with the "Down Perishables", a train that was fully fitted with vacuum brakes. The station was still well endowed with seats and gaslights in the mid-1950s. (R.S.Carpenter)

74.   A glimpse of the goods yard is obtained from platform 1 on 5th March 1960, as no. 6028 *King George VI* races south, with steam issuing from embarrassing parts. The goods traffic ceased on 6th July 1964. (P.C.Wheeler)

75.   The 1933 signal box was built on the south-west side of the line and its 74-lever frame was in use until 1st September 1969. New sleepers are stacked on the platform between the relief lines, which were abandoned in 1968. (Lens of Sutton coll.)

76.   A 1972 photograph reveals that the LMR staff removed almost all traces of GWR enterprise. The brackets on the massive screen for the doorway to the gents once carried well groomed fire buckets. (H.C.Casserley)

77.   Recent renovation schemes included erection of a canopy on the down side and the end, ornamental tiling of the waiting room and provision of a buffet. On the negative side was withdrawal of long distance trains on 18th May 2003. An example is the Virgin CrossCountry Voyager, which is passing through non-stop on 8th November 2003. (V.Mitchell)

78. Seen on the same day is the east elevation which had been generally enhanced and provided with an example of modern art. More useful was a bus interchange behind the camera. (V.Mitchell)

OLTON

79. The quadruple track shown at the top of the next map came into use to Tyseley on 27th January 1907. Its junction signal box is in the background of this photograph. The one on the right is also shown on the map, but was redundant by then. The locomotive appears to be a "Badminton" class. (Lens of Sutton)

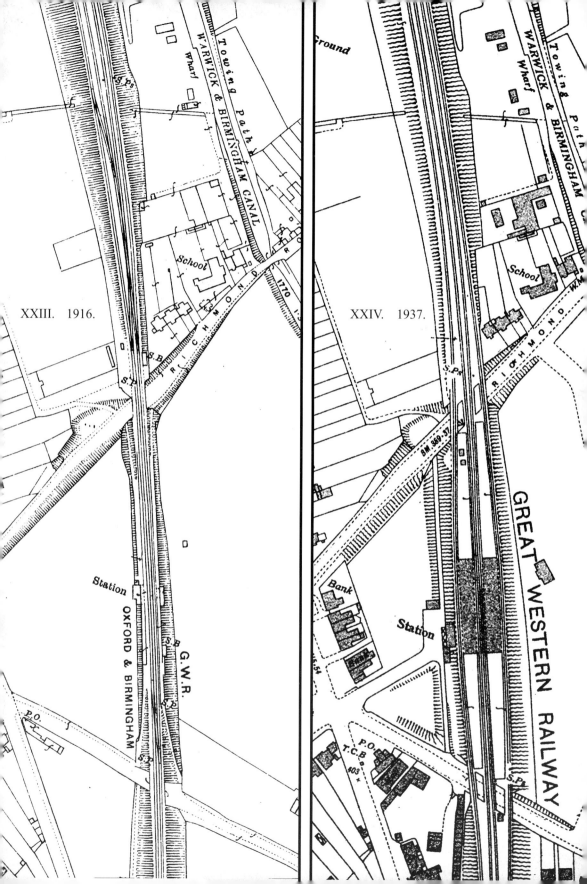

XXIII.   1916.

XXIV.   1937.

80. The original station opened in 1869 and was demolished to make way for two standard island platforms in 1933. The staff of 11 in 1923 was reduced to 7 by 1935. (Lens of Sutton)

81. The original four inclined footpaths gave way to an approach road and subway in 1933. The entrance and booking hall were recorded in 1948. The new signal box had 31 levers and lasted until 1969. (R.S.Carpenter coll.)

82. No. 4096 *Highclere Castle* heads a northbound express of Southern Region stock in August 1962. The fire buckets were most commonly used to deal with smouldering sleepers. The two buildings on the left platform remained in 2003, linked by a flat roof. (J.H.Moss/R.S.Carpenter)

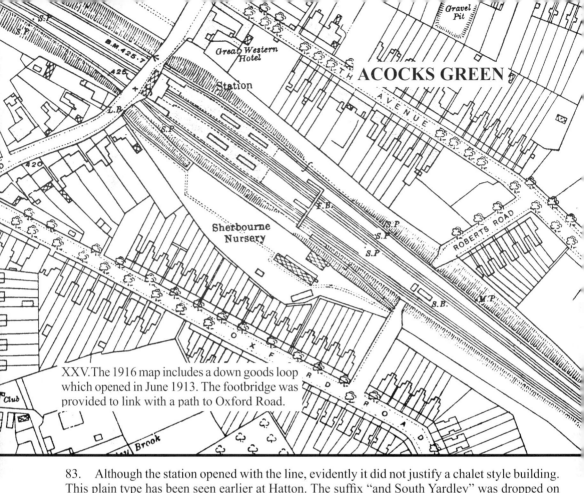

ACOCKS GREEN

Great Western Hotel

Station

Sherbourne Nursery

ROBERTS ROAD

Gravel Pit

OXFORD ROAD

Brook

Club

XXV. The 1916 map includes a down goods loop which opened in June 1913. The footbridge was provided to link with a path to Oxford Road.

83. Although the station opened with the line, evidently it did not justify a chalet style building. This plain type has been seen earlier at Hatton. The suffix "and South Yardley" was dropped on 8th May 1968. (Lens of Sutton)

84. The island platforms were provided with the standard buildings, but the down main starting signals were offset as seen, owing to the track curvature. There were usually 13 men employed here between the wars. (Lens of Sutton)

85. An LMR class 5 4-6-0 runs north on the down main with an express from the South Coast in about 1964. The signal box had 33 levers and was in use from 1907 to 1969. (A.W.V.Mace/Milepost 92½)

86. The main entrance was photographed in 1963 and the ticket office was still in use 40 years later. However, at platform level there was only a bus shelter. (J.H.Moss/R.S.Carpenter)

TYSELEY

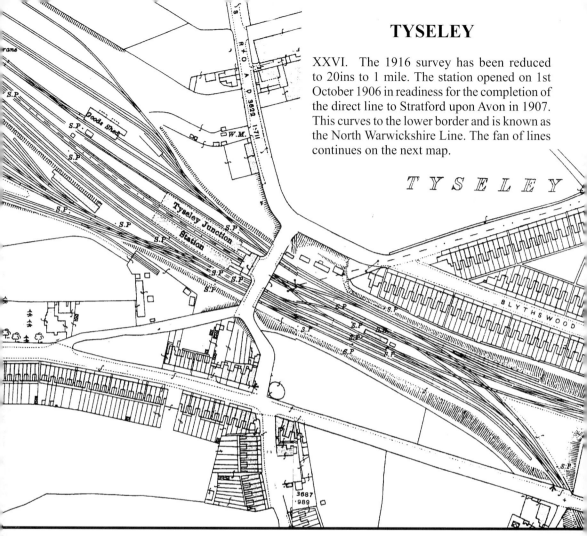

XXVI. The 1916 survey has been reduced to 20ins to 1 mile. The station opened on 1st October 1906 in readiness for the completion of the direct line to Stratford upon Avon in 1907. This curves to the lower border and is known as the North Warwickshire Line. The fan of lines continues on the next map.

87. A southeastward postcard view confirms that the usual GWR building plans were employed and it includes the signal box, which was close to the junction. The staff numbered over 70 for goods and passenger work from the opening, up to World War II. This excluded loco and shed staff. (Lens of Sutton)

88.	Two views east from the road bridge on which the main building stands feature the junction, the North Warks route being on the right. This photo is from 29th July 1961 and features no. 5014 *Goodrich Castle* with a train from that line passing Tyseley South box, which had 136 levers and worked until 1st September 1969. (G.Adams/M.J.Stretton coll.)

89. The junction was greatly simplified in 1968 to the form seen in this photograph from 15th May 1976. It remained unchanged in 2003. This stopping train for Birmingham Snow Hill has just passed under the centre arch. (T.Heavyside)

90. The south elevation is seen in November 2003, not long after the premises had been renovated. The ticket office was still staffed. Out of view in the left background had been the goods yard until 9th September 1968. Two sidings were retained for loading cars. (V.Mitchell)

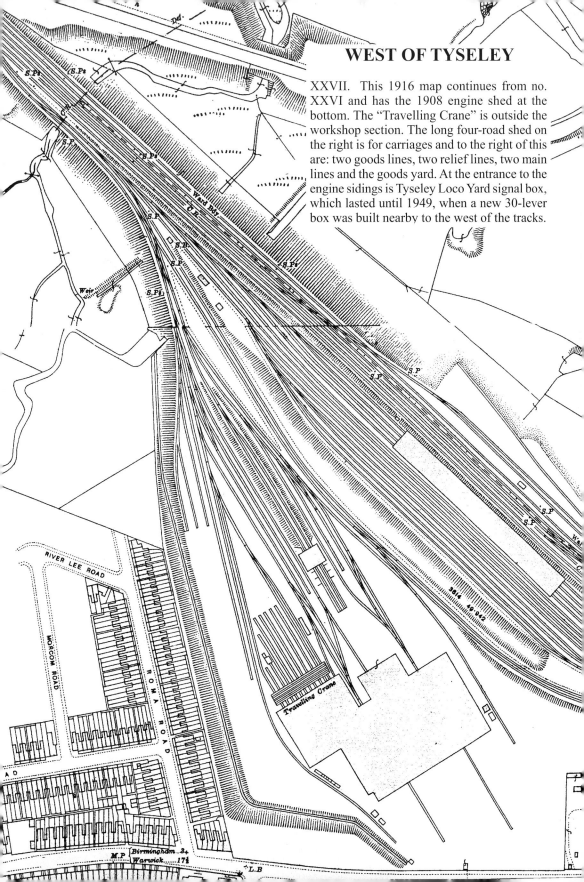

WEST OF TYSELEY

XXVII. This 1916 map continues from no. XXVI and has the 1908 engine shed at the bottom. The "Travelling Crane" is outside the workshop section. The long four-road shed on the right is for carriages and to the right of this are: two goods lines, two relief lines, two main lines and the goods yard. At the entrance to the engine sidings is Tyseley Loco Yard signal box, which lasted until 1949, when a new 30-lever box was built nearby to the west of the tracks.

91. The term "Factory" was used by the GWR to describe their main repair workshops, which were usually (as here) adjacent to a large running shed. This view from September 1948 includes the internal overhead travelling crane. (R.S.Carpenter)

92. In the left background of this 1951 picture is the engine shed, which contained two 65ft turntables from each of which radiated 28 bays. To the right of 4-4-0 "Bird" class no. 3454 *Skylark* is the two-road coal stage, which is represented as a square on the map. The shelter on the left was a wartime addition to minimise glare from fire dropping. There were about 100 engines based here in the mid-1950s, this reducing to 55 by 1963, when the shed code changed from 84E to 2A. Steam ended here in November 1966 with just three 0-6-0PTs allocated. (R.S.Carpenter)

93. Total dieselisation of local services began during 1957 and part of the fleet was recorded at rest on a Sunday in April 1982, the location being at the centre of map XXVII. The main line is on the high ground on the left; the lower lines are to the diesel locomotive depot and the Birmingham Railway Museum. The two Engine Loops are beyond the stacks of bricks. (T.Heavyside)

XXVIII. The origin of the Birmingham Railway Museum can be traced to 1967 when Mr. Pat Whitehouse purchased no. 7029 *Clun Castle* and no. 5593 *Kolhapur*. He housed them in the coal stage and the museum developed from this nucleus in the 1970s on the adjacent site. The old engine shed had been demolished, but the northern turntable and its associated lines remained.

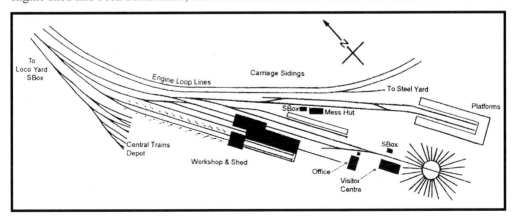

94.   New workshop buildings were erected close to the coal stage, which is still surmounted by a water tank. *Kolhapur* was in its original 1934 livery when pictured on 4th April 1982. (T.Heavyside)

95.   Seen on the same day is "Pannier" no. 7752 of 1930, with the rear bogie of its train on the turntable. Scrap steel is no longer loaded in the siding on the left and the museum uses all the land up to it. Two platforms were built in that area and up to four tour trains per annum leave for trips on the national system, using the museum's GWR liveried train. This is used on the "Shakespeare Express" to Stratford upon Avon from Birmingham. (T.Heavyside)

96.   Track alterations were in progress when no. 5080 *Defiant* was photographed on 16th July 1987. The site is operated by Tyseley Locomotive Works Ltd and has since become congested with stock awaiting restoration. The steam locomotives included in 2003 two other "Castles", three "Halls", three 0-6-0PTs and three others. There were about 12 diesels, some industrials and more than 30 coaches. They are usually on view at weekends, but confirmation by telephone is advised. (BRM/CMW)

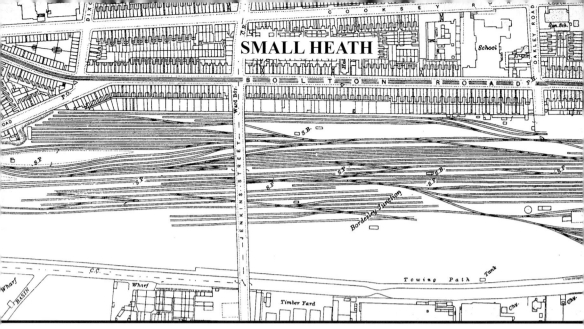

SMALL HEATH

XXIX. The 1918 survey at 15ins to 1 mile has the station and Small Heath North box on the right page and Bordesley Junction box on the left one. Bordesley Sidings box is above it. The single line curving up on the left was Midland Railway property and linked the GWR to the MR line from Gloucester to Birmingham New Street. Most of Small Heath goods yard is on the right page, while all of Bordesley goods yard is on the left. General traffic ceased on 6th July 1964, but many of the sidings were retained as "Caledonia Yard" for motor vehicle traffic. Four became part of a coal concentration depot. There had been an engine shed here before Tyseley opened. The two signal boxes were replaced by Bordesley South, which had 181 levers and was in use from 30th November 1913 until 1st September 1969.

97.   No. 5104 runs in with a local service from Birmingham Snow Hill to Leamington Spa on 13th July 1956. In the background is Small Heath North box which functioned from about 1912 until 1969. (R.S.Carpenter)

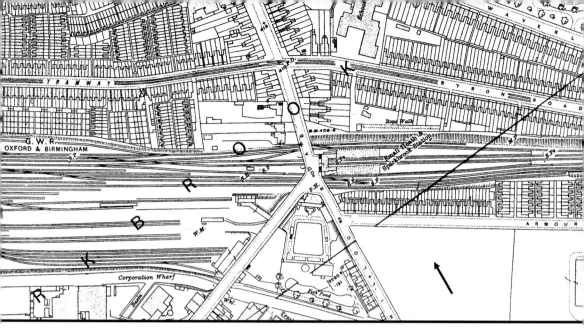

98. No. 6998 *Burton Agnes Hall* and no. 5900 *Hinderton Hall* ran tender-first from Tyseley to Saltley prior to returning a special train to their base at Didcot on 15th May 1976. All four platforms were still functional, as at Tyseley, in 2003. (T.Heavyside)

99.   No. 47012 is approaching the station on 15th May 1976 with the 15.21 Liverpool to Southampton service. The space on the right was once covered with sidings; they remain on the left bearing carflats. Jenkins Street strides across the picture. (T.Heavyside)

100. Moving further west, we see two trains on Bordesley Curve, with another on the skyline on the former MR main line. The DMU is new and is being delivered to Tyseley from Derby on 14th September 1957. The curve had been doubled in 1941 and has been used by North-South expresses since their transfer from Snow Hill to New Street. (G.Adams/M.J.Stretton coll.)

101. We have now passed under the main line from Gloucester and witness no. 3673 pulling out of the goods yard on its way to Snow Hill and Hockley Yard. It is approaching Bordesley station. (G.Adams/M.J.Stretton coll.)

BORDESLEY

XXX.   The station opened in 1855 and is shown on the 1918 edition, which was surveyed during major alterations which began in 1915. In March, the first of two island platforms came into use and a fifth track for down goods followed. Land for the extra tracks is shown each end of the station, which has two platforms and a bay. Bordesley Station box is shown; it was replaced by Bordesley North which was north of the tracks and west of the junction. It had 47 levers and closed on 1st September 1969. The goods shed was demolished during the alterations and cattle pens were built on part of its site. The viaduct curving north from the shed was completed in 1853 and was intended to carry a link with the LNWR. However, this was never laid and it only ever bore a headshunt. Duddeston Viaduct still stands today as a monument to the politicians who took 150 years to recognise the need for a Strategic Rail Authority.

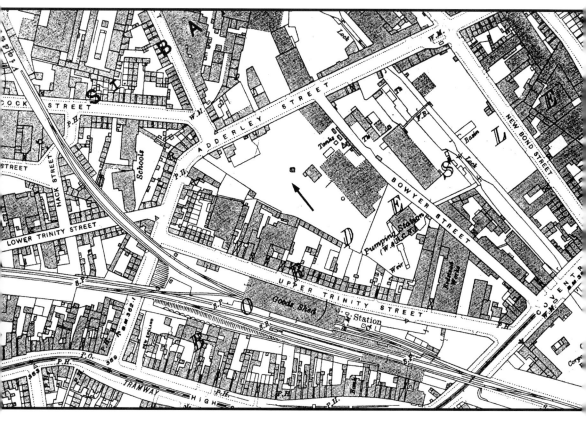

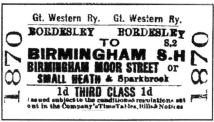

102. This eastward panorama was taken from the bridge in the background of the previous picture in about 1955. Within ten years, all the cattle wagons on the right would be redundant. The platforms are in the distance and a coal train is on the down goods line. This was out of use from 1973 to 1977, when it was reinstated as a reversible line, which was still in use in 2003. (R.S.Carpenter)

103. The original entrance was south of the station, in the High Street (see map). The entrance to the booking hall is in deep shadow in this 1964 picture. From it, two staircases gave access to the platforms. There was a staff of 11 or 12 in the 1930s, employed mainly on freight, which ceased on 6th July 1964. (R.M.Casserley)

104. This 1964 eastward view includes the girders of the bridge over Adderley Street and the bridge carrying the Gloucester line is in the mist in the distance. Note that the platforms are staggered. The southern one was in use in 2003, devoid of buildings, but there were only two trains calling: the 07.48 to Stourbridge Junction and the 17.05 to Shirley. (R.M.Casserley)

BIRMINGHAM MOOR STREET

XXXI. The 1918 edition at 20ins to 1 mile was surveyed earlier, during the construction of the station. Only half the station and part of the trackwork is complete. Pictures 106 and 107 show the finished scheme. Our route crosses the page and enters the 596yd long Snow Hill Tunnel on the left of it. Below these lines the LNWR tracks enter two tunnels, which pass under the concourse of Moor Street on their way to New Street.

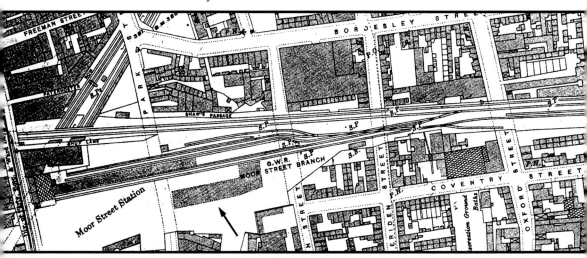

105. The station opened on 1st July 1909. The steepness of Moor Street is evident in this 1951 view, which includes part of the tramway which served the city from 1904 to 1953. City status was granted in 1889. The BR sign was unorthodox. (LGRP/NRM)

106. A westward panorama from the signal box on 17th May 1958 shows no. 6014 *King Henry VII* on the down main. The relief lines diverge to join the main lines or enter Moor Street. On the right is the up goods line and a siding. This viaduct is more than ½ mile long. Duddeston Viaduct is in the left background. (R.S.Carpenter coll.)

107. A view towards the buffers includes all four platforms and the goods shed, which opened on 7th January 1914. The yard had seven sidings, the southern ones being at a low level. Goods traffic ceased on 6th November 1972. Locomotives were released from the nearest three lines by traversers. These two units were scrapped in 1967 and one crossover was put in just beyond the locomotive. (Lens of Sutton)

108. No. 6340 is taking a parcels train from the down relief to the down main line on 1st July 1959. The main lines eastward were taken out of use on 5th March 1967 and the route to Snow Hill followed on 2nd March 1968. The 1909 box had 118 levers and closed on 1st September 1969, along with many others. Their work was transferred to Saltley Panel. (R.S.Carpenter)

109. A notable transformation took place on 28th September 1987 when Snow Hill tunnel and station reopened. Two new platforms were built at Moor Street, the remaining three terminal ones were closed and the relief lines slewed to join the new ones. The 1909 station is in the background as the 12.16 Shirley to Stourbridge Junction arrived on 8th November 2003. The next four pictures were taken that day to show more good news. (V.Mitchell)

110.   The listed buildings remained unused and neglected until restored to GWR style and standards by Chiltern Railways in conjunction with Birmingham Alliance, developers of the nearby Bullring shopping centre. This attracted 1.5m visitors in its first four days in September 2003 and the revitalised terminal buildings were officially opened on 11th October. (V.Mitchell)

111.   A new ticket office was provided on the concourse, but the 1987 one (centre) was retained above the up platform. It is at the north end of the footbridge, which was scheduled for repositioning and provision of lifts. The illuminated sign did not promote the railway. (V.Mitchell)

112. The GWR ambience is enhanced by the traditional signs, although platforms 3 to 5 were not in use. There is direct access to platform 1, the opening in the wall being evident in picture 109. The stairways to the footbridge can be seen through the railings. (V.Mitchell)

113. To advertise the regular steam-operated "Shakespeare Express" to Stratford upon Avon, 2-8-0 no. 2885 stands at platform 5 with a banner on the Bullring side of its boiler. The locomotive belonged to the GWR Preservation Group Ltd of Southall, but was not in working order. The train is operated by Vintage Trains Ltd on most Summer Sundays, but has run from Snow Hill as reconnection of the tracks to these platforms from the running lines was delayed. (V.Mitchell)

BIRMINGHAM SNOW HILL

XXXII. The 1918 survey reveals that much of the station was roofed over and that the site was constrained regarding development. There are tunnels at each end and a canal under the middle. The line climbed at 1 in 45 from Moor Street and so a larger ventilation hole was provided in the station roof at the south end.

114. The first major development was the construction of the GWR's hotel at the south end of the station in 1863. Initially the station had two through platforms and one bay. (Lens of Sutton)

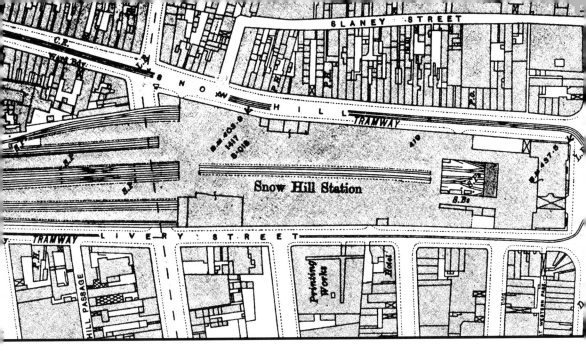

XXXIII. The next important change took place in 1871, when more bay platforms were added.
Note the wagon turntables on the sidings under the hotel and the central footbridge.

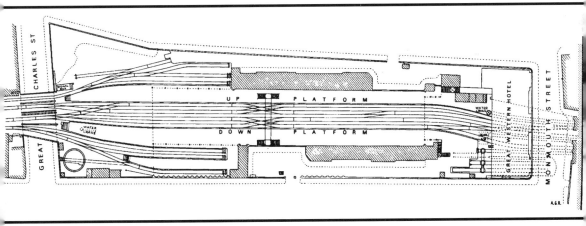

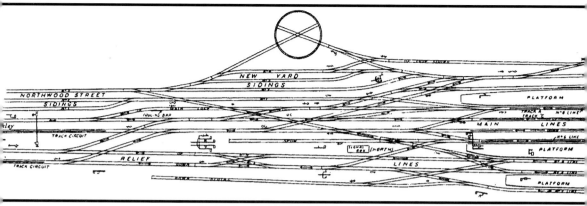

XXXIV. The final rebuild took place in 1905-13, when the through platforms were greatly lengthened and doubled in number. The location of North Box (224 levers) is outside the station, but South Box (96 levers) is effectively in the tunnel, as are many sidings. The levers were miniature ones operating electrically powered equipment.

115. No. 3294 *Blenheim* of the "Badminton" class was photographed during the reconstruction. Over 6000 tons of iron and steel were used in the mighty roof and its supports. More than one train could use the down main platform simultaneously under a special "permissive working" arrangement. There were special "asking" procedures with the two boxes to the south, to enable trains to rush the gradient in the tunnel under clear signals.
(R.S.Carpenter coll.)

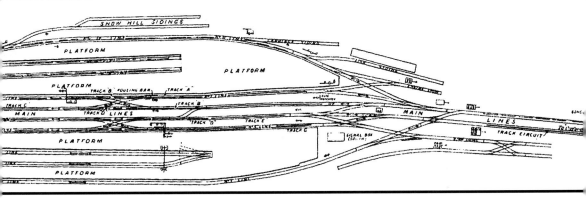

116. This montage was produced by the GWR to impress all with the scale of their astonishing achievements. The total effective platform length had been trebled, but it was still congested at times and hence the need to create Moor Street to relieve pressure on this national rail centre. Top left - up main and relief platforms; top right - north end; lower left - up and down main; right - up main platform. (GWR Magazine)

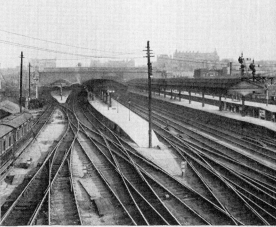

117. No. 5040 *Stokesay Castle* and no. 5049 *Earl of Plymouth* are about to enter the fumes of the tunnel on 19th October 1961. To add to their density, the station pilot engine often stood on the short siding inside the tunnel. A curious tuneless gong, immortalised on a gramophone record in 1935, was sounded erratically by a wheel treadle to help drivers know their location in the asphixiating gloom of smoke, dust and steam in the apparent attempt to create railway hell in the tunnel. (A.W.V.Mace/Milepost 92½)

118. The common hectic atmosphere prevailed on 27th April 1963 as class 8F no. 48417 and an SR Bulleid "Pacific" head a football special, while no. 34094 *Morthoe* waits to work another. Freight was often held here awaiting a path through the tunnel, where double track restricted flow. (A.W.V.Mace/Milepost 92½)

119. The great cathedral of God's Wonderful Railway suffered a slow and miserable decline, despite great protestations from its worshippers. As stated, the tunnel closed on 2nd March 1968 and the station was not staffed after 5th May 1969. DMUs from Wolverhampton, often a single car, terminated here until total closure on 4th March 1972. Use as a car park followed and demolition began in 1976. It proved difficult - the Nazis had failed. (Lens of Sutton)

120. The creation of the West Midlands Passenger Transport Executive in 1969 brought positive thinking and four platforms came into use on 5th October 1987. The one on the left was lost to trams from Wolverhampton in 1999, restricting railway capacity, although at Wimbledon they share one platform, end-on, successfully. The trams run through no. 4 to their own low platforms. The gloomy new station requires the permanent use of artificial lighting in its most used area. The 12.10 to Marylebone waits to leave on 8th November 2003. The Edwardian enterprise in transport matters seems to have been reinvented in Birmingham, despite some evidence of Modern Mismanagement Methods. (V.Mitchell)

Middleton Press

Easebourne Lane, Midhurst, W Sussex. GU29 9AZ Tel: 01730 813169 Fax: 01730 812601
Email: sales@middletonpress.co.uk   www.middletonpress.co.uk
If books are not available from your local transport stockist, order direct post free UK.

BRANCH LINES
Branch Line to Allhallows
Branch Line to Alton
Branch Lines around Ascot
Branch Line to Ashburton
Branch Lines around Bodmin
Branch Line to Bude
Branch Lines around Canterbury
Branch Lines around Chard & Yeovil
Branch Line to Cheddar
Branch Lines around Cromer
Branch Line to the Derwent Valley
Branch Lines to East Grinstead
Branch Lines of East London
Branch Lines to Effingham Junction
Branch Lines around Exmouth
Branch Lines to Falmouth, Helston & St. Ives
Branch Line to Fairford
Branch Lines to Felixstow & Aldeburgh
Branch Lines around Gosport
Branch Line to Hayling
Branch Lines to Henley, Windsor & Marlow
Branch Line to Hawkhurst
Branch Line to Horsham
Branch Lines around Huntingdon
Branch Line to Ilfracombe
Branch Line to Kingsbridge
Branch Line to Kingswear
Branch Line to Lambourn
Branch Lines to Launceston & Princetown
Branch Lines to Longmoor
Branch Line to Looe
Branch Line to Lyme Regis
Branch Line to Lynton
Branch Lines around March
Branch Lines around Midhurst
Branch Line to Minehead
Branch Line to Moretonhampstead
Branch Lines to Newport (IOW)
Branch Lines to Newquay
Branch Lines around North Woolwich
Branch Line to Padstow
Branch Lines to Princes Risborough
Branch Lines to Seaton and Sidmouth
Branch Lines around Sheerness
Branch Line to Shrewsbury
Branch Line to Tenterden
Branch Lines around Tiverton
Branch Lines to Torrington
Branch Lines to Tunbridge Wells
Branch Line to Upwell
Branch Line to Wantage (The Wantage Tramway)
Branch Lines of West London
Branch Lines of West Wiltshire
Branch Lines around Weymouth
Branch Lines around Wimborne
Branch Lines around Wisbech

NARROW GAUGE
Austrian Narrow Gauge
Branch Line to Lynton
Branch Lines around Portmadoc 1923-46
Branch Lines around Porthmadog 1954-94
Branch LIne to Southwold
Douglas to Port Erin
Douglas to Peel
Kent Narrow Gauge
Northern France Narrow Gauge
Romneyrail
Southern France Narrow Gauge
Sussex Narrow Gauge
Surrey Narrow Gauge

Swiss Narrow Gauge
Two-Foot Gauge Survivors
Vivarais Narrow Gauge

SOUTH COAST RAILWAYS
Ashford to Dover
Bournemouth to Weymouth
Brighton to Worthing
Dover to Ramsgate
Eastbourne to Hastings
Hastings to Ashford
Portsmouth to Southampton
Ryde to Ventnor
Southampton to Bournemouth

SOUTHERN MAIN LINES
Basingstoke to Salisbury
Crawley to Littlehampton
Dartford to Sittingbourne
East Croydon to Three Bridges
Epsom to Horsham
Exeter to Barnstaple
Exeter to Tavistock
London Bridge to East Croydon
Orpington to Tonbridge
Tonbridge to Hastings
Salisbury to Yeovil
Sittingbourne to Ramsgate
Swanley to Ashford
Tavistock to Plymouth
Three Bridges to Brighton
Victoria to Bromley South
Victoria to East Croydon
Waterloo to Windsor
Waterloo to Woking
Woking to Portsmouth
Woking to Southampton
Yeovil to Exeter

EASTERN MAIN LINES
Barking to Southend
Ely to Kings Lynn
Ely to Norwich
Fenchurch Street to Barking
Hitchin to Peterborough
Ilford to Shenfield
Ipswich to Saxmundham
Liverpool Street to Ilford
Saxmundham to Yarmouth
Tilbury Loop

WESTERN MAIN LINES
Banbury to Birmingham
Bristol to Taunton
Didcot to Banbury
Didcot to Swindon
Ealing to Slough
Exeter to Newton Abbot
Moreton-in-Marsh to Worcester
Newton Abbot to Plymouth
Newbury to Westbury
Oxford to Moreton-in-Marsh
Paddington to Ealing
Paddington to Princes Risborough
Plymouth to St. Austell
Princes Risborough to Banbury
Reading to Didcot
Slough to Newbury
St. Austell to Penzance
Swindon to Bristol
Taunton to Exeter
Westbury to Taunton

MIDLAND MAIN LINES
St. Albans to Bedford
Euston to Harrow & Wealdstone
Harrow to Watford
St. Pancras to St. Albans

COUNTRY RAILWAY ROUTES
Abergavenny to Merthyr
Andover to Southampton
Bath to Evercreech Junction
Bath Green Park to Bristol
Bournemouth to Evercreech Junction
Brecon to Newport
Burnham to Evercreech Junction
Cheltenham to Andover
Croydon to East Grinstead
Didcot to Winchester
East Kent Light Railway
Frome to Bristol
Guildford to Redhill
Reading to Basingstoke
Reading to Guildford
Redhill to Ashford
Salisbury to Westbury
Stratford upon Avon to Cheltenham
Strood to Paddock Wood
Taunton to Barnstaple
Wenford Bridge to Fowey
Westbury to Bath
Woking to Alton
Yeovil to Dorchester

GREAT RAILWAY ERAS
Ashford from Steam to Eurostar
Clapham Junction 50 years of change
Festiniog in the Fifties
Festiniog in the Sixties
Festiniog 50 years of enterprise
Isle of Wight Lines 50 years of change
Railways to Victory 1944-46
Return to Blaenau 1970-82
SECR Centenary album
Talyllyn 50 years of change
Wareham to Swanage 50 years of change
Yeovil 50 years of change

LONDON SUBURBAN RAILWAYS
Caterham and Tattenham Corner
Charing Cross to Dartford
Clapham Jn. to Beckenham Jn.
Crystal Palace (HL) & Catford Loop
East London Line
Finsbury Park to Alexandra Palace
Holborn Viaduct to Lewisham
Kingston and Hounslow Loops
Lewisham to Dartford
Liverpool Street to Chingford
London Bridge to Addiscombe
Mitcham Junction Lines
North London Line
South London Line
West Croydon to Epsom
West London Line
Willesden Junction to Richmond
Wimbledon to Beckenham
Wimbledon to Epsom

STEAMING THROUGH
Steaming through Cornwall
Steaming through the Isle of Wight
Steaming through Kent
Steaming through West Hants

TRAMWAY CLASSICS
Aldgate & Stepney Tramways
Barnet & Finchley Tramways
Bath Tramways
Brighton's Tramways
Bristol's Tramways
Burton & Ashby Tramways
Camberwell & W.Norwood Tramways
Clapham & Streatham Tramways
Croydon's Tramways
Dover's Tramways
East Ham & West Ham Tramways
Edgware and Willesden Tramways
Eltham & Woolwich Tramways
Embankment & Waterloo Tramways
Exeter & Taunton Tramways
Fulwell - Home to Trams, Trolleys and Buses
Great Yarmouth Tramways
Greenwich & Dartford Tramways
Hammersmith & Hounslow Tramways
Hampstead & Highgate Tramways
Hastings Tramways
Holborn & Finsbury Tramways
Ilford & Barking Tramways
Kingston & Wimbledon Tramways
Lewisham & Catford Tramways
Liverpool Tramways 1. Eastern Routes
Liverpool Tramways 2. Southern Routes
Liverpool Tramways 3. Northern Routes
Maidstone & Chatham Tramways
Margate to Ramsgate
North Kent Tramways
Norwich Tramways
Reading Tramways
Seaton & Eastbourne Tramways
Shepherds Bush & Uxbridge Tramways
Southend-on-sea Tramways
South London Line Tramways 1903-33
Southwark & Deptford Tramways
Stamford Hill Tramways
Twickenham & Kingston Tramways
Victoria & Lambeth Tramways
Waltham Cross & Edmonton Tramways
Walthamstow & Leyton Tramways
Wandsworth & Battersea Tramways

TROLLEYBUS CLASSICS
Bradford Trolleybuses
Croydon Trolleybuses
Derby Trolleybuses
Hastings Trolleybuses
Huddersfield Trolleybuses
Hull Trolleybuses
Maidstone Trolleybuses
Portsmouth Trolleybuses
Reading Trolleybuses

WATERWAY & SHIPPING
Kent and East Sussex Waterways
London to Portsmouth Waterway
Sussex Shipping - Sail, Steam & Motor
West Sussex Waterways

MILITARY BOOKS
Battle over Portsmouth
Battle over Sussex 1940
Blitz over Sussex 1941-42
Bombers over Sussex 1943-45
Bognor at War
East Ridings Secret Resistance
Military Defence of West Sussex
Military Signals from the South Coast
Secret Sussex Resistance
Surrey Home Guard

OTHER RAILWAY BOOKS
Index to all Middleton Press stations
Industrial Railways of the South-East
South Eastern & Chatham Railways
London Chatham & Dover Railway
London Termini - Past and Proposed
War on the Line (SR 1939-45)